ZOOLOGICAL MEMOIRS

ZOOLOGICAL MEMOIRS

Alexis Komenan

Copyright © 2024 Alexis Komenan
All rights reserved.

ISBN: 978-2-955-47495-2

Illustrations: Alexis Komenan

Introduction

I am Ivorian, born in 1986. I live a grown-up life like everyone else. Like all my human brothers and sisters, I struggle to live and contribute to the well-being of my family and society. My childhood was everyone's childhood. Well, almost! Besides friends, school, games, football, Formula 1, drawing, in short everything you can imagine, how many are those who have unfortunately not experienced the joy, the feeling of being close to nature and animals in a very special way?

For I had the privilege of observing or even establishing a strong relationship with a diversity of animal characters, both wild and domestic, some raised in family or elsewhere, and the others, cosmopolitan, present on their own. To name a few, these singular friends diversified into chickens, agamas, antelopes, turtles, brush-tailed porcupines, cats, squirrels, guinea pigs, dogs, sheep, goats, mongooses, pangolins, pigeons and turtledoves, herons and ravens, passerines, monkeys, ants, monitors and even crocodiles.[1]

---

[1] In all the localities where we lived, I observed or raised the following types at home: chickens, antelopes, turtles, brush-tailed porcupines, sheep, turkeys, guinea fowls, ducks, cats, mongooses, goats, pangolins, squirrels, guinea pigs, monitors, etc. a bit quails. Dogs, pigeons and especially agamas and turtledoves are

These pages are therefore a collection of observations of this mysterious and captivating world of animals, which I made during my childhood. Such interesting experiences have left enough of their mark on my young age to immortalize their memory, a little like men such as Jean-Henri Fabre and his *Souvenirs entomologiques*.

It would have been interesting to put the observations of so many species on paper. But apart from the first five mentioned, unfortunately, not all the others will be the subject of it in the short term, because their observation was average or sporadic, or because the memories were insufficient. The same is true of agriculture and the vegetable world, which I also loved very much. As I plan to produce a collection only devoted to chickens, I will honor only the following four species in this document.

---

everywhere, as well as the inevitable and friendly passerines of various species. Not to mention bats. In this category of "off-road," we will not forget the herons and ravens. Kites are also relatively visible, as are many other birds such as touracos or, until a few years ago, screech owls and coucals. We know that insects, including the interesting ants, are everywhere. I also raised crickets in Bingerville. I have observed oxen, ducks, rabbits, monkeys, etc. at friends' houses or elsewhere. As for the crocodiles, they were at the lakes of Yamoussoukro and in the enclosure of the minor seminary of Saint-Augustine of Bingerville. I had also the opportunity to observe, for the first time, many of the country's wildlife species and peacocks in semi-freedom at the Abidjan Zoo.

It would be unfair to share with others the memory of these little four-legged comrades without devoting a note to my semi-aquatic turtle of the *Pelusios* type, which was given to me by a friend of the village a few good years ago and which disappeared, I don't know how, in late 2011.

Except for the section on the *Pelusios* and the paragraph on second-generation land turtles, all other parts were put in writing in 2002. I simply reviewed, corrected and completed them here and there in 2012. I also made some minor corrections in 2015.

The Land Turtles

Generic name: Land Turtle
Scientific name: *Kinixys* (sp.); *Testudo* (sp.)
Habitat: sheltered, discreet (heaps of dead leaves...) and wet areas of forests and savannahs
Diet: vegetarian, but adapts to an omnivorous diet. Fruits, some creeping plants, lettuce, mushrooms, wet bread, raw or cooked plantain, plant flowers, eggs
Habits: poorly known. Swimming occasionally. Can fast for a long time
Longevity in captivity: exceeds three years
Observation period: from 1997 to 2010

When I owned my first turtle, I didn't know what to give it. So I accidentally tried wet bread. He ate it. Then I dropped him off in the courtyard - it was in Bingerville. He walked around it and found two main shelters: one at the foot of a bushy ornamental plant, and the other between two stems of climbing plants, the space being covered with dead leaves. I realized the turtle was a very discreet animal that could adapt perfectly to its environment. He therefore lived in hiding, only coming out during the rains, and receiving the above mentioned food. Then a second smaller land turtle was brought to me. After feeding him, I placed him next to the first one in order to detect social behavior in the habits of these still insufficiently known animals. The first one, being the largest, took out his head and went in the little one's direction, who deviated so as not to meet the other's trajectory. I knew then that there could be a social hierarchy among turtles. In the first few days, they ignored each other, but gradually each one got used to the other, because they had the same territory and the same dormitories. They often rested together, next to each other, and when I distributed earthworms to them, I could appreciate the social behavior of these animals: as the tallest one approached, the shortest one deviated when he came in or gave up his prey to avoid getting caught, which happened if he didn't comply. Observing them was even more interesting because they were two different species, but they had the same habits...

In 2001, my father brought me a new turtle - the first two mentioned having disappeared some time earlier, the biggest one dead of ascariasis,[2] the

---

[2] They were white worms about 3 to 5 cm long, which she kept vomiting one day. It was in Riviera Palmeraie. Later, I suspected, rightly or wrongly, some parasite probably present in the snails in the garden, which she consumed, to be at the origin of the fatal disease.

other one no longer found. It was a male - after him, my friend from the village offered me the freshwater turtle. A few years later, two other land turtles followed: a female belonging to my elder brother's friend, and another male, returning from a trip of the parents, a little later. As soon as the female arrived, the first dominant male had a great time! So we saw, much later, two newborns walking in the garden, but who then disappeared, we don't know how.

So, for the following land turtles, I gave up seeing meat on their menu.

The African Mud Turtle

Generic name: African Mud Turtle
Genus: *Pelusios*
Habitat: amphibious (bush streams and water points, sheltered areas on adjacent banks)
Diet: carnivorous (earthworms, animalcules, small fish, pieces of meat or fish, in captivity). Omnivorous too, according to specialists
Habits: day and night (in captivity). Enjoys swimming and therefore enjoys the temporary pools formed by the rains
Longevity in captivity: indefinite, but exceeds five years
Observation period: 2004-2005 to 2011

Pelusios or *Pelomedusa*? The distinction was not at all clear in the research, until I remember that the front part of my turtle's breastplate was removable, which is a feature of the first kind cited.

The *Pelusios* is a very endearing animal, with a smiling snout, which showed fear during the first moments of its arrival, but got used to people and me as I got to know it. Of a discreet naturalness on the whole, like all turtles, he could be a biting bitch when he saw me coming, walking towards me, examining my hands and feet and trying to bite, probably thinking she was dealing with edible food! Being able to recognize me at a good distance when he saw me or when I looked at him, he could come and follow me until he got satisfaction, a small portion of fish (fresh detritus or cooked piece) or, more rarely, meat. But of course he also managed on his own - I was no longer as available to animals as I used to be, several years ago - finding earthworms and other small animals in the water here and there. So the rainy weather was a real recreation for him, as he swam like never before, the air visibly happy, in one of the spacious temporary pools created during the rain, especially the pond on the edge of the terrace of our kitchen. It should be noted that on observation, the *Pelusios* feeds only in water, which makes it easier to grab and maneuver its food or prey, which is very difficult for it to do on land. The slightest rain was an excuse for her to go out. He would then retire, looking either in the courtyard or in a room of the house (kitchen, terraces, garage) for a place sheltered enough to rest there. It could stay in this way for several days, if not several months, closed or semi-closed shell, suggesting a lethargic entry. He lived with my second generation land turtles with whom he shared the same range territory and dormitories -

including the former brush-tailed porcupines plank house. It was a rather good agreement, although *Pelusios* suffered many chases from the dominant male, so territorial, in his early days. His small circular eyes were quite expressive: I could read the good mood, satisfaction, or even a certain melancholy of the animal. We really enjoyed each other. When the rain was scarce, I would put him according to my availability - and when he too hadn't been holed up - in an old tub or something else containing water, to keep him company, feed him and hydrate him a little.

I haven't seen him since the end of 2011. Is it disappearance in reason of heavy rains? Exit or removal? I don't know. However, when, on rain occasions, the pond in front of the kitchen terrace, being formed, desperately searches for a swimmer, I of course remember its famous tenant to whom I dedicate these lines.

The Red-Flanked Duiker

Generic name: Red-Flanked Duiker
Scientific name: *Cephalophus rufilatus*
Habitat: thickets, bushes and other discreet areas (in the forest area)
Diet: leaves, flowers, roots, tubers, tender bark and young shoots, some fruits and sometimes sweets (in captivity or in the wild). Vegetarian
Habits: nocturnal (sometimes daytime, in captivity)
Longevity in semi-free captivity: six years, perhaps more
Observation period: 1991 to 1997

Grace, vivacity and mistrust characterized the young female duiker that was given to us by a family friend and named after Mina.[3]

---

[3] She was named after an antelope from a French book in primary school.

As soon as she arrived, after freeing herself from the embrace of the man who had brought her in, she ran to hide behind the climbing plants bordering the fence, which formed almost impenetrable rows of thickets. She stayed there, so as not to be seen by men, for a few days, perhaps only going out at night. Finally, she quickly got used to the human presence and her new environment, an extremely large garden, with not only grass and ornamental plants but also many trees, and a termite mound reminiscent of the wilderness. The animal had every reason to be satisfied with an environment that was so conducive to animal husbandry. As a result, it walked around there day and night, eating all kinds of plants. Nevertheless, Mina received from us meals made of cassava, plantain, vegetables, and our attachment. To return to her habits, it is important not to exaggerate the importance of her movements in the yard, whether they are daytime or nighttime, because, exactly as in the forest, the animal spent most of its time napping in the bushes and went out, but especially at dusk, to indulge in a game known to many animals, running training.[4] And she was growing up.

As an adult, she was brought from Bouaké a male named Péko, donated by an aunt, but who unfortunately died of injuries while struggling in the car that carried him. His horns were more

---

[4] Sometimes "titillated" by mongooses, cat and even, once or twice, by the neighbor's bitch...

pointed than those of his female, and the latter did not seem to pay him any attention, at least on the surface. She would stand at a distance and then approach, as if to comfort him, and then leave. She had totally gotten used to men.

My observations on Mina showed me that these animals can only survive in captivity with large areas containing grass, bushes and tall trees, as in the bush, and not places that are certainly vegetated but too cramped for these ruminants, as in Bingerville, where she finally became ill, having no bushes or extensive gardens... Here, I think I have said everything, at least the most essential, about the life of wild ruminants like the duiker in captivity.

The Brush-Tailed Porcupine

Scientific name: *Atherurus africanus*
Common name: Hedgehog [5] (by the Ivorian populations)
Habitat: sheltered areas (dead trees, fallen tree trunks, crevices, holes) of forests and forest savannahs
Diet: vegetarian (leaves, roots, fruits, bread, cereals, soybeans, peanuts)
Habits: nocturnal. Swimming occasionally
Longevity in semi-free captivity: over two years
Observation period: from 1998 to 2000

The observations I made on my two brush-tailed porcupines showed me that these animals, although a little fearful, get used to humans and can even distinguish them in captivity.

---

[5] The brush-tailed porcupine is often likened to the real hedgehog (*Atelerix*), which is rather insectivore and lives in the north of the country.

As soon as they arrived home in July 1998 (my father brought them to me when he returned from his trip), and still young, I placed them in a box with hay and food. But after two days, they fled from this dwelling and found in a pile of boards and wood in the courtyard, a safe home exactly like their wild habitat. There, they managed on their own, feeding on a certain plant familiarly called "mamichou" that grew spontaneously in the yard, and whose leaves are commonly used in sauces. The papaya flowers that fell to the ground also made up their menu. Very intelligent,[6] they arranged galleries and "spaces" through their board habitat, which then benefited other animals, namely turtles, lizards and agamas and the cat.

I discovered them on the fourth day since they left the cardboard house. From then, besides their resourcefulness (yard plants, kitchen peels), I fed them and they became attached to me. They distinguished me from the other people in the court. They feared them a little, but with me, it was different. They could harass me until they got

---

[6] I often tested them by burying groundnut pods or some other food in the ground in front of them, sometimes attracting them to it, to see if they would keep their instinct for resourcefulness. They showed it to me admirably by locating the food, thanks to their sense of smell. All they had to do was to dig.
I also grew peanuts in the garden. Unlike our chickens, who ate the seeds, they left most of the plants until the pods matured: once I woke up and was amazed to discover my first field completely devastated, and the plants amputated of their pods! But I didn't hold it against them...

some food, waiting for me even when I went to get it, as if they knew I would come back. These animals had adapted very well to captivity. Strangely enough, they never left the house, even when at night, to my great fear, the gate was open, because they recognized their territory. When they felt threatened, they would adopt a fighting posture, raising their fearsome thorns, making the silks of their tails shiver and become nervous. It was the black and white cat of the court that provoked them. These mini-fights between porcupines and cat were spectacular. Thus, one night, we heard noises like machine gun shots. We were in a period of military transition. As I looked around, I realized it came from the dome of boards, transformed into a field of explanations for the occasion. It was actually the brush-tailed porcupines who, with a good dose of animal black humor, compressed their bodies that produced this noise aimed, once again, at intimidating the cat. But the cat, teasing, didn't disband. The biggest porcupine then went for him, thorns spiked, but the feline, not to be stung, jumped without clumsiness on a board to meow ferociously in their direction. And the little battle resumed again, with insignificant scratches on each side... In the end, the two species got along quite well despite the disputes, because they shared the same board house. The brush-tailed porcupines used their powerful orange incisors to gnaw at the hard wood in order to carve their way. Looking at their habitat, I noticed it was complex: there were two large piles of wood close together and they arranged in both. There were rooms to sleep in, to keep food, to defecate and to rest during the sunny hours. They also used their strong little legs to dig into the ground and enlarge their homes. It was the cohabitation in harmony with the other tenants of the plank house, including my two smaller guinea pigs, who enjoyed their company.

Robust, careful in their movements but very agile, the brush-tailed porcupines could not reproduce, because they were females. It would have taken a male to create a family, given their remarkable adaptation to captivity in semi-liberty. The only flaw in these rodents was their habit of gnawing. Accused by mistake of having damaged an external part of Dad's car during the year 2000 - it was actually mice -, they were put to death, to my great dismay, but after having confused their pursuers, my elders, by feints in their race!

Brush-tailed porcupines, like many animals, control the growth and texture of their claws and teeth by "sharpening" them on the wood. They also design their shelters to manage rainwater runoff and leave a strong odor characteristic of their territory. They also had the curious habit of swallowing some of their droppings, perhaps to recover nutrients. Like all animals used to humans, they were not afraid to visit the rooms of the house!

And again, I noticed that sometimes one would go in search of food while the other would stay in place, apparently to guard the den. They only fully engaged in their night activity when all the lights were off, their eyes shining in the dark.

Thus, *Atherurus africanus*, the animal that eats food in both hands, what am I saying, between its two front legs, has shown a fine example of domestication and adaptation of wild animals to the domestic state, under certain minimal living conditions. So I think I've said the essential things about the lives of these rodents in captivity.

The Agama

Scientific name: *Agama agama*
Common name: Margouillat (in French)
Habitat: human neighborhood for the anthropophile type (cities and villages, unfinished or abandoned houses, fields); wilderness for the wild type
Food: insects, earthworms, leftover foods, plants. Omnivorous
Habits: Daytime
Longevity: indefinite
Regular observation period: from 1994 to 1997

Agamas, commonly known as "margouillats" in French, are reptiles, cold-blooded animals. There are two types: the so-called anthropophile type (who lives near man) made up of those found everywhere. Adult males have a head that varies in color from pale yellow to bright orange to almost red; the wild type, not very different from the first, but some individuals are said to have a green head.[7] I will only talk here about the anthropophile type, the one which is best known to me.

They are most often seen plastered on house fences or tree branches to heat in the sun in order to capture the rays needed to maintain their body temperature. A short head, sturdy legs, a tapered tail characterizes agamas, and their general appearance evokes small monitors or small crocodiles at a faster rate. Other no less important characteristics of agamas are their very observant eye, their agility, the bright colors of the male and especially the inevitable head signs. There is a significant sexual dimorphism in the species, males being more robust, more colorful, while females are smaller and dull. The young ones, from the first few months of their lives, have all the same coloring, a more or less brown color on their bodies and a greenish brown spotted on their heads. As they grow older, the distinction becomes clearer, with young males being greenish brown, at least dull, but generally more robust than adult females.

My observations have also shown me that there is, as in all social animals, a hierarchy established in a group of agamas. Each male has an adequate

---

[7] The difference I knew between the anthropophile type and the wild type is in the tail's color: while the wild agama has a ringed blue appearance, the anthropophile agama is often tricolored (blue-orange-black).

territory, which he travels through and on which he basks with his family. It is also in this area that mating takes place. Generally, all the territories of the dominant ones are contiguous, one being a neighbor of the other. Males in their territory are on their guard, either to locate an enemy or to intimidate and drive away rivals. When two males meet at the limits of their respective territories, they can engage in spectacular duels, although they are of short duration. It is simply a matter of alerting the neighbor so he does not encroach on the other's territory. But these "explanations" can sometimes be prolonged. Thus, in the family yard in Bingerville, I could see several of these hot clashes between the dominant ones, including an epic duel that, I remember, lasted from the afternoon, between 2 p.m. and 3 p.m. there, at about 6 p.m., both males, who knew each other "very well," wanting to fight it out because they had a lot on their hearts! In a fight between two agamas, each one stands parallel to the other. They bend their tails horizontally on the side opposite the opponent, reveal their erectile organ at the neck, switching, for males, from the normal blue-black and orange color to a "fight" color, gray on the body, dark on the head. They then give each other merciless tail strikes and bites, returning to their marks, chin swollen, mouth open to collect oxygen during the fight, delaying, intimidating, restarting the attack again or dodging to counterattack. When the battle is over, the two opponents, especially the males, returned to their territories and regained their normal color, stopping regularly to nod. The nodding of the head is one of the major characteristics of agamas. Males in particular, young or adult, cannot make a movement without stopping for head signs. They have several functions because we find them in all areas of the life of these reptiles. For my part, I have distinguished, in all age and gender categories combined, seven different ways of nodding. They show the mood, satisfaction, submission, mistrust, nervousness, or even the social rank of the individual.

Adult male landowners defend their possession not only against their neighbors but also against young mature males in search of territory. Equally memorable battles are fought, which can last for hours, until the defeated, often the old male, leaves the territory still in "sportswear" while the winner already establishes himself in the colors of the dominant. But mostly, when they have no possession, young males, taking on a dull hue that characterizes neutrality, wander from one territory to another. In the presence of the place's master, the young male is discreet, dull by color, and when the former approaches him, he lifts the tip of his tail and nods discreetly, as a sign of submission. The individual deemed suspicious by the owner of the premises is chased away by a chase. Some of these "squatters" are sneaky: they pretend to be submissive in the presence of the dominant, but once the latter is out of sight, they take on the normal colour and temporarily become the leaders.

When the males court the females by biting their backs, they pretend to free themselves and raise their tails. They lay eggs in a carefully chosen site on the ground, then cover the dug hole with soil. At the end of the incubation period, the young hatchlings live more or less discreetly - like all young people, they do not escape gaming - until they reach maturity.

Agamas are rather peaceful animals, although they may seek to bite to free themselves when grabbed, their jaws being pricked with tiny pointed teeth, like those of real lizards.

Large predator of invertebrates of all kinds, although they do not disdain men's leftover meals, agamas can react very quickly when they feel danger. This does not prevent them from having predators that enjoy eggs, young and adults alike. These are cats and other small carnivores, raptors, sometimes crows, snakes, and even humans. Agamas are day animals. At night, they rest in the crevices of trees and walls, in the bric-à-brac, in one word in sheltered and hard-to-reach places. Here I have given the main part of the life of the agamas near man.

Conclusion

There is still much to be said about this world so interesting - for initiates - of animals. But I am no longer a child, and I no longer really have the leisure for caring of animals or study them. Availability is lacking. I still have other interests that, however, we must be assured, have not canceled my interest in the natural world.

Many children in the cities of the current younger generations have little or no contact with nature. As a result, our little classmates sometimes ignore even the names of the most high-profile species! We have not to ignore nature for the sole benefit of human distractions or of dealing with it almost exclusively, to the detriment of socialization. But knowing the surrounding creatures, besides being entertaining and informative, can help us protect them, live in better harmony with them and enjoy them better in these times of environmental degradation and animal scarcity. It is in our interest, theirs and the planet's.

My experience with the species mentioned here has also shown me, and this is important, that it is better to abstain from pets when there is insufficient or no time, resources or science to deal with them. This applies to both wild animals and domestic animals, which is a matter of the health and safety of the animal and the owner himself[8]. But also for convenience: animals prefer to roam around in the open air more comfortably than to stay in cages all the time, that's for sure.

We still remember with pleasure all those friends with legs or fins. They have enriched our human experience. Let us greet them and all those who have allowed us to know them and pay tribute to the incomparable genius that, somewhere, inspires all these wonders we enjoy.

---

[8] This will avoid the suffering of the animal and the risk of contagion for humans, if inexperience in this area or if it is impossible to consult a veterinarian. Even if some diseases disappear on their own after a while, such as for the two brush-tailed porcupines who, a few months after their arrival, were victims of a parasitic furunculosis from which they fortunately cured afterwards, it is not clear how.

www.ingramcontent.com/pod-product-compliance
Lightning Source LLC
Chambersburg PA
CBHW061518040426
42450CB00008B/1683